Exotic
FRUITS & FLOWERS
IN NEEDLEPOINT

Exotic
FRUITS & FLOWERS
IN NEEDLEPOINT

STELLA KNIGHT

Guild of Master Craftsman Publications Ltd

First published 2005 by
Guild of Master Craftsman Publications Ltd,
166 High Street, Lewes,
East Sussex, BN7 1XN

Please note: thread colour codes refer to the threads used in the projects as shown in the photographs.
The charts and keys should be regarded as reference only.
Threads used in this book are supplied by Anchor, a subsidiary of Coats.
Thread colour codes therefore refer to Anchor/Coats threads only.
A Thread Conversion Chart for the equivalent threads in DMC and Madeira is printed on page 126 of this book.

ISBN 1 86108 471 4

A catalogue record of this book is available from the British Library.

Managing Editor: Gerrie Purcell
Production Manager: Hilary MacCallum
Project Editor: Clare Miller
Designer: John Hawkins

Typeface: Berkeley Book and Skia

Colour origination by Wyndeham Graphics

Printed and bound in Singapore by Kyodo Printing

To my family

CONTENTS

CULTIVATED CROPS

AMERICAS

INTRODUCTION

Tropical plants and trees are found in regions around the planet where the climate is wet and humid and there is little seasonal change. The abundant rainfall with high temperatures and humidity give rise to evergreen forests in which there is continuous plant growth undisturbed by cold or drought. The tropics is contained within the two imaginary belts that encircle the earth; the Tropic of Cancer, located at 23° 27' north, and the Tropic of Capricorn, located at 23° 27' south of the Equator. In this area the sun is directly overhead at least once, and often twice a year. The difference between the summer months and the winter months is barely noticeable. Even on the shortest day the tropical sun shines for ten and a half hours.

Conditions in the tropics are very different from those that people living in moderate latitudes are used to. Almost constant temperatures and relatively stable length of days permit year-round growth of plants as long as enough water is available. However, the lack of cold in the winter months makes plants more vulnerable to pests. The amount of solar radiation and amount of evaporation is more than twice as high as it is in more moderate climates.

Soil conditions are also of special importance to the flora. Soil in the Northern Hemisphere appeared after the last ice age and is less than 10,000 years old. In the tropics, many landscape surfaces have been exposed to weathering for millions of years. Weathering in the tropics is essentially more intensive than in the moderate latitudes. Often the nutrient-binding minerals of clay were destroyed long ago, and rain washed out the nutrients. What remains is the typical red, tropical soil that, when dried out, can turn into rock-hard laterite.

The luxuriant vegetation of these soils remains alive only through constant recycling. When the dead parts of plants rot, actinomycetes absorb the nutrients before they can enter the soil. Thus the plants receive nutrients from the bacteria rather than from the soil. If this cycle is interrupted, many nutrients are lost for good. Young soils, rich in nutrients are found in the tropics in meadows close to rivers and in places where volcanoes have deposited their lava. Ironically agriculture flourishes best in places where people are seriously threatened by flooding and volcanic eruptions.

Within the tropics there is a wide diversity of environments. There are Rain Forests, Deciduous Forests, Mountainous Forests, Savannas and Mangroves. High mountain regions as well as lowland desert areas are included and all this gives an overwhelming variety of plant species. Approximately 200,000 plant species are at home in the tropics. Some of these are so rare that few people have seen them, while others are far more common but are camouflaged in their forest habitat and some are conspicuous enough for the casual observer to notice. These are the species that I have selected as lending themselves well to the bold patterns and glowing colours of needlepoint.

I have also tried to choose plants that are colourful. In the tropics the predominant colour is green – albeit many, many shades of green! Flowers are relatively rare in relation to the amount of foliage, so a plant needs to be bright if it is to be noticed by a potential pollinator. The colours that show up most against green foliage are those which contrast most strongly, especially reds, oranges and yellows, through to magenta and bright pinks. Totally blue flowers are rare. It is likely that 10–15% of the Earth's flowering plants have not yet been described. Most will be in the moist tropics especially remote parts of Latin

America. Brazil is the country which is believed to have the most plant species (56,000), followed by Colombia (35,000), China (30,000) and further down the list, Tropical Africa (10,000). The rainforests of South-east Asia are home to the largest flowers on Earth. The biggest individual flowers are those of *Rafflesia arnoldii*, a parasitic plant from Sumatra and Borneo with fleshy, basin-shaped flowers 39½in (100cm) across. This flower is designed to attract insects that enjoy carrion, which means it has a truly awful smell! Unfortunately the Rafflesia is threatened by habitat loss and over-collection.

In this book I have tried to incorporate as many colours and shapes as possible to give a variety to the designs. Strong geometric shapes such as the Globe Artichoke contrast strongly against the flowing Chinese Honeysuckle. The abundant flowers in the Pink and Blue Tropical Flowers cushion and the Wild and Cultivated Flowers cushion are very different from the Calla Lily cushion or the Cayenne Peppers cushion.

MATERIALS AND TECHNIQUES

The art of embroidery can be traced back to the Middle East, around AD500, where it was passed from the Persians to the Greeks. The King of Pergamus is said to have been one of the first to have used gold thread, and the women of Sidon were renowned for their embroidery skill. Needlepoint is a form of embroidery in which stitches are used to cover an open canvas. Also known as canvas-work embroidery, it became popular in the eighteenth century, when ladies embroidered designs on canvas fabric using woven tapestries as an inspiration.

Embroidery stitches may be functional or purely decorative. Decorative stitches are known by such names as chain stitch, blanket stitch, featherstitch and French Knot. I have tended to use the basic half cross stitch for the designs in this book, although I have used French Knots in the Coconut Bookmark and a cross stitch in the Chinese Honeysuckle Cushion. I have also tended to use wool thread for the majority of the designs, although in some, notably the Malaysian Orchid Tree cushion, I have included some stitches in stranded cotton. Stranded cotton adds a sheen and, when used amongst the wool, it gives an added lustre.

Needlepoint is a most rewarding pastime and there is so much you can create. Not only is there the pleasure that comes from making something beautiful, there is also the satisfaction of seeing the finished article and knowing that it will be admired for many years. As with gardening, you need patience, but when the plant grows and the flowers appear, whether in the garden or on canvas, you get an immense feeling of satisfaction.

MATERIALS

Canvas

Needlepoint is stitched on a cotton fabric called 'canvas'. This fabric is woven to resemble a mesh, allowing the needlepoint stitches to be worked through the holes. The canvas is usually found in two forms: either single threads woven, called 'interlock canvas', or two fine threads woven together, called 'double-thread canvas'. Generally the interlock canvas can be found in a finer quality; that is, there are more holes to the inch. This is ideal for detailed designs, especially where silks or stranded cottons are used instead of wool.

In this book I have tended to use 12-hole interlock canvas. I find that this is ideal for giving a good amount of detail to the design, but it is also fairly quick to stitch. A large design stitched using a fine canvas can take so long to complete that it is sometimes never finished!

A good tip is to cover the edges of the canvas with masking tape. This stops the canvas catching your clothes.

Frames

Frames are useful when stitching a needlepoint design, as they tend to stop the work distorting. However, if you tend to take your design on journeys it may be better to work without a frame. If you do find that your work is lopsided when finished, this can easily be remedied by ironing the back of the needlepoint with a hot steam iron and gently pulling the work back into shape. This may need to be done several times.

Frames can be easily purchased from embroidery or hobby shops and come in a variety of shapes and sizes.

Needles

The proper needle to use for needlepoint is one that has a blunt end. They come in all sorts of sizes, but my favourite is a size 20. It can be used with most canvases. In embroidery or haberdashery shops these needles tend to be known as 'tapestry needles'.

Threads

Wool is the main thread used here. I tend to use Anchor Tapisserie Wool, which is readily available worldwide. There is a chart later in the book converting the Anchor colour numbers to DMC and Paterna, just in case the Anchor colours are hard to find. Wool is hard-wearing and durable so the finished needlepoint should last for many, many years.

With some of the designs I have also added some stranded cotton threads. These threads have a sheen and lustre which the wool lacks, and just add an extra interest to certain designs.

If your design gets dirty it is very easily cleaned by either gently sponging it with soap and water, ensuring that the work is not soaked, or by using a good upholstery spot-clean dry cleaner.

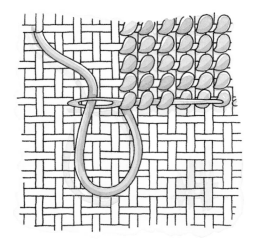

TECHNIQUES

Starting and finishing

The correct way to begin stitching is to pass the needle through the canvas a little way away from where you want to begin to stitch. Hold some of the wool firmly and then move the needle to where you want to stitch. After working several stitches take the yarn end to the wrong side and secure it by passing it through the back of several stitches. This will hold it firmly in place.

To finish the yarn, either when the yarn is near its end or when a certain part of the design is completed, pass the needle through the back of a few worked stitches.

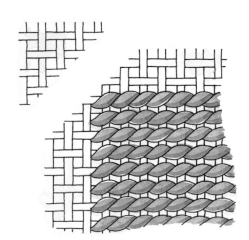

Cutting corners

Cutting the corners diagonally stops a build-up of canvas when the work is finished and made up. Just be careful not to snip too close to the worked stitches!

Stretching the finished needlepoint

This needs to be done when the needlepoint has been worked without using a frame, as you will find the piece of work distorted. It is very easy to do, and you can be quite firm.

First of all, dampen the back of the work with some water. Try not to soak the embroidery. Using a hot steam iron, tug at the work while ironing – on the back of the work – and gradually the needlepoint will begin to get back into shape. If you find that the work is still not quite right, then repeat after leaving it to dry completely.

For work that is very misshapen, iron with a hot steam iron as before, and while it is still damp tack to a wooden board covered with a clean tea towel in the shape you want it. Leave to dry completely – usually overnight – unpin, press lightly with an iron and the embroidery should be in shape.

Backing a cushion

The needlepoint should be backed with a fairly thick fabric. I tend to use upholstery velvet, which is available in a wide variety of colours.

Either by hand or by machine lay the embroidery on the backing fabric with right sides facing. Pin around the edges to hold it in place. Start stitching two inches in from the bottom left-hand corner and continue around the three sides until you are about 2in (5cm) in from the bottom right hand corner. This ensures all the four corners have been sewn and should give you a good gap to stuff the cushion pad.

Trim the four corners by cutting the material diagonally then trim any excess canvas and material around the cushion.

Turn the work the right way round, stuff with a cushion pad and sew up the gap. Any trimmings can then be added if required.

A zip can be added, which is best done after pinning but before sewing around the four sides.

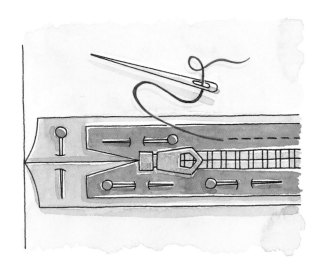

STITCHES

Half cross stitch

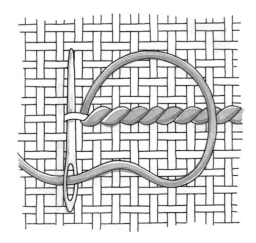

This stitch is used the most for needlepoint and can be worked from right to left or left to right. It is important that all the stitches slope in the same direction on the front. On the back of the work the stitches should be vertical.

Tent stitch

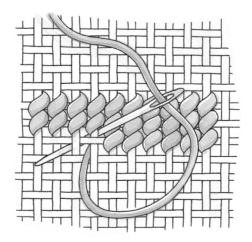

This is also used a lot in needlepoint and makes the embroidery more hard-wearing than the half cross stitch as both the front and back of the work have sloping stitches. It does use up a lot more wool though.

French Knots

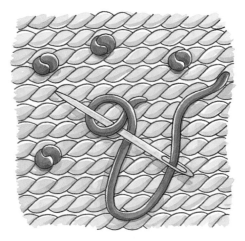

These are very easy to do and can be quite effective. Bring the yarn to the front of the canvas in the required position, hold it firmly with your thumb, make a loop, pass the needle through the loop and pull through. Take the excess yarn to the back of the work. You may want to practise the stitch once or twice to get the right tension.

Long-armed cross stitch

This is a wonderful stitch to use when joining the backs and fronts of embroidered pieces of work, such as pincushions or spectacles cases. It makes a very neat edge. It is similar to cross stitch, but you work two stitches forward and one back, which ensures all the canvas is covered.

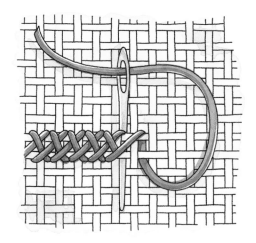

Slip stitch

This is used when wishing to back a piece of embroidery with lining fabric, or when closing the gap after stuffing a cushion. An ordinary sewing needle is used – one with a sharp point. When worked properly the stitches should be invisible.

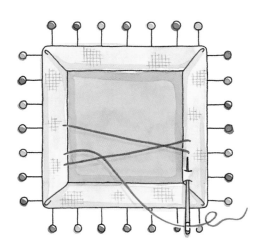

Lacing for framing

Many of the designs in this book can be turned into pictures by mounting them on a board and framing them. When the embroidery is finished and pressed, cut a piece of board to a size just slightly smaller than the finished work. Secure the embroidery to the board with pins pushed into the edges, stretching it smoothly and tightly as you work. Then lace the unworked pieces of canvas together, first horizontally, then vertically, starting in the centre and working towards the corners. For a good even result the laces should be fairly close to each other.

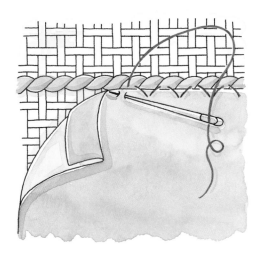

ASIA

In Asia the tropics cover a wide area including western India, Sri Lanka, parts of the Malaysian region and an area from the Himalayas in the north extending into Indo-China and the Philippines. The tropics are also found across an area extending from New Guinea to Fiji and southwards into northeastern Australia. With temperatures between 20 and 30°C and high levels of rain, plants grow quickly. In Southeast Asia, one family of plants, the dipterous fruit plant, dominates the great trees of almost every forest. Because there are no seasons in the humid rainforests, the trees that grow there can bloom and sprout at any time throughout the year. Many of these trees grow 80–100ft (24–36m) high and some have been recorded as being 230ft (70m) high. In one 24¾-acre (10-hectare plot) of Malaysian rainforest 780 tree species were found, which is more than the total number of tree species native to the USA and Canada combined.

Asia lost almost a third of its tropical forest cover between 1960 and 1980; the world's highest rate of forest clearance. In 1988 the great floods of Thailand alerted the government to the dangers of forest clearing. A study carried out on the effects of deforestation found that a forested slope subject to landslides lost 0.03 tons of soil per 2½ acres (1 hectare) per year, whereas for a deforested slope the loss was 138 tons of soil per 2½ acres (1 hectare) per year. You can also add to this the carbon dioxide that is released into the air when forests are burnt. Forests that are burnt will not resume their previous life, as the ground is no longer fertile enough for trees to grow; it will be like a house gutted after a fire. What's more, the heavy rains that hit the forests – normally up to 80in (200cm) a year – will sit on the ground and flood the area, causing mud and landslides. The Ganges Plain in India is the most densely populated region in the world. It has suffered severe flooding because of deforestation.

PINK AND BLUE TROPICAL FLOWERS CUSHION

MATERIALS

- 1 piece of 10-hole double-thread canvas, size 20 x 20in (50 x 50cm)
- 1 skein each of wool colours 8622, 8114, 8690, 8216, 8220, 9006, 9172, 8296
- 2 skeins each of wool colours 8006, 8396, 8644, 9076
- 5 skeins each of wool colour 9800
- Backing fabric
- Cushion pad

Wonderful hibiscus, vibrant morning glories and charming white rhododendrons make up this glorious cushion. As well as a host of beautiful flowers which fill the air with wonderful perfume, there are often beautiful birds and insects, some that are just as colourful. Approximately 80 per cent of all insect species live in tropical rainforests, as does the largest flower on Earth, the rafflesia, which grows up to 3ft (1m) across. In some highland areas the temperatures can fluctuate greatly within a day. During the day the sun warms up the soil while at night temperatures can drop to freezing point, though this is only in areas above 13,000ft (4,000m).

INSTRUCTIONS

= 9172
= 9076
= 9800
= 8644
= 8396
= 8690
= 8114
= 8006
= 9006
= 8296
= 8220
= 8216
= 8622

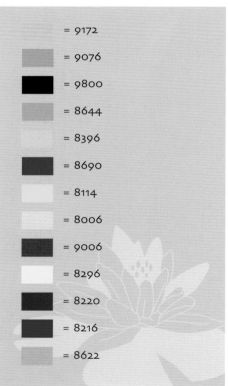

1 Follow the chart to work the design, starting from the middle. Use half cross stitch throughout.

2 Press the embroidery on the back with a hot steam iron over a damp cloth and gently pull it back into shape. If it is still not straight dampen it again, pin it to a wooden board covered with a tea towel and leave to dry overnight.

3 With right sides together, sew the backing fabric to the embroidery on three sides.

4 Trim any excess canvas and fabric to within 13mm ($\frac{1}{2}$ in). Also cut the corners diagonally.

5 Turn right sides out and insert the cushion pad.

6 Close the open seam with a slip stitch.

A black and white version of this chart, which can be enlarged on a photocopier for easier working, can be found on p116

MALAYSIAN ORCHID TREE CUSHION

MATERIALS

- 1 piece 12-hole canvas size 20 x 20in (50 x 50cm)
- 1 skein each in wool colours 8490, 8526, 8488, 8394, 8404, 8342
- 2 skeins in wool colours 8484, 9800, 9020, 9100, 9096
- 6 skeins in wool colour 8006
- 1 skein stranded cotton colour 2
- Backing fabric
- Cushion pad

MEDINILLA MAGNIFICA
FAMILY: MELASTOMATACEAE

This stunning tree originally came from the Philippines and can grow up to 10ft (3m) high. The leaves are heart-shaped and slightly leathery while the flowers are up to 1in (2.5cm) long. They are pink, red or a light violet. Medinilla is used as an ornamental plant and, even in the tropics, is seen more often in a pot than in a garden. It is difficult to spot in the wild, preferring to grow in the forks of the branches of large trees. There are approximately 400 Medinilla species growing but most do not have the striking bracts of the Malaysian orchid tree. However, they are very similar, and varieties can be found almost everywhere in the tropics.

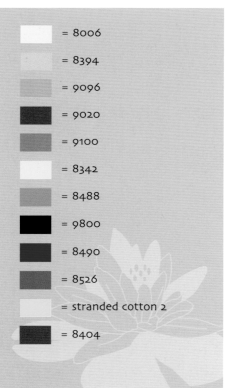

	= 8006
	= 8394
	= 9096
	= 9020
	= 9100
	= 8342
	= 8488
	= 9800
	= 8490
	= 8526
	= stranded cotton 2
	= 8404

INSTRUCTIONS

1 Follow the chart to work the design, starting from the middle. Use half cross stitch throughout.

2 Press the embroidery on the back with a hot steam iron over a damp cloth and gently pull it back into shape. If it is still not straight dampen it again, pin it to a wooden board covered with a tea towel and leave to dry overnight.

3 With right sides together, sew the backing fabric to the embroidery on three sides.

4 Trim any excess canvas and fabric to within $\frac{1}{2}$ in (13mm). Also cut the corners diagonally.

5 Turn right sides out and insert the cushion pad.

6 Close the open seam with a slip stitch.

A black and white version of this chart, which can be enlarged on a photocopier for easier working, can be found on p117

CHINESE HIBISCUS PINCUSHION

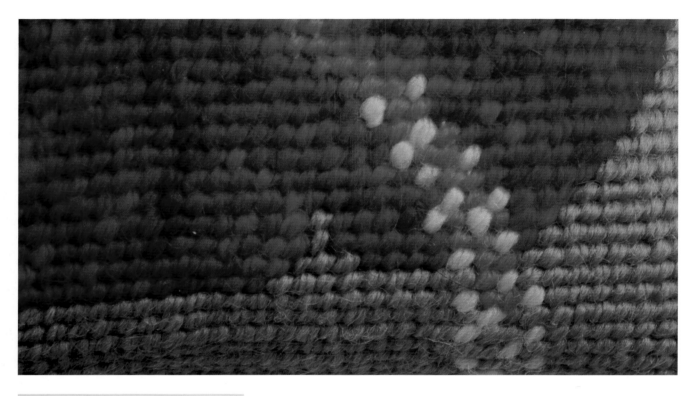

MATERIALS

- 2 pieces 12-hole interlock canvas size 8 x 8in (20 x 20cm)
- 1 skein each in wool colours 8198, 8216, 8218, 8354, 8006, 8114, 8168
- 2 skeins in wool, colour 9098
- Stuffing

HIBISCUS ROSA-SINENSIS
FAMILY: MALVACEAE, MALLOW PLANTS

This plant has a stunning flower and is one of the most popular ornamental bushes of the tropics and subtropics. The flowers are large and often bright red, with five undivided petals and one midrib which has many yellow anthers in the upper third. Originally from Southeast Asia it has been cultivated in Asia for a very long time. For many years, people used the juice of its flowers to blacken the colour of their hair, eyebrows and even shoes. The plant can grow up to 20ft (6m) high and the flowers are often 4–6in (10–15cm) wide. Besides the wild specimens there are many cultivated versions in a multitude of colours.

▨	= 8114
▨	= 9098
▨	= 8168
▨	= 8216
▨	= 8218
▨	= 8198
▨	= 8354
▢	= 8006

INSTRUCTIONS

1 Follow the chart to work the designs, starting from the middle. Use half cross stitch throughout.

2 Press the embroideries on the back with a hot steam iron over a damp cloth and gently pull them back into shape.

3 Trim any excess canvas to within ½in (13mm) and cut the corners diagonally.

4 Fold the unworked canvas to the wrong side all the way round.

5 With right sides facing out (wrong sides together), join the two pieces using a long-armed cross stitch starting just before one corner. Stitch almost all the way round leaving a gap about 2in (50cm).

6 Stuff the pincushion and finally stitch the gap continuing the long-armed cross stitch.

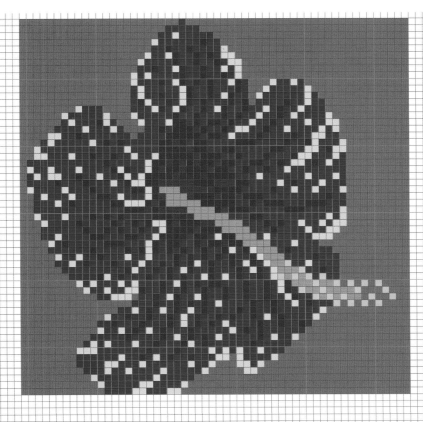

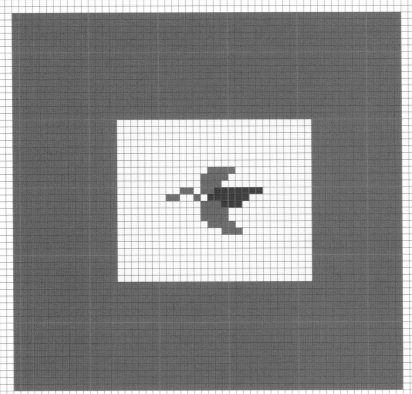

CHINESE HONEYSUCKLE CUSHION

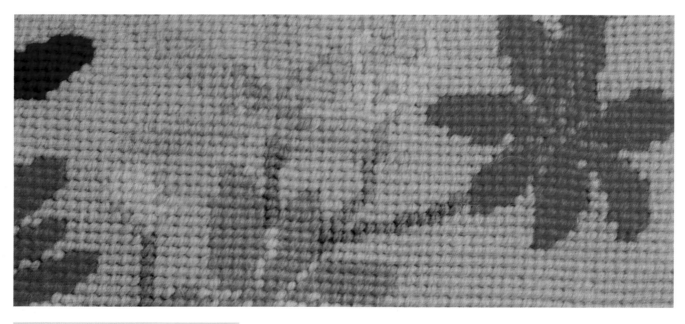

MATERIALS

- 1 piece 12-hole interlock canvas size 23 x 23in (60 x 60cm)
- 1 skein each of wool colours 8232, 8404, 8058, 9100
- 2 skeins each of wool colours 8434, 8394, 8212
- 3 skeins each of wool colour 9096
- 4 skeins each of border background wool colour 9442
- 10 skeins each of background wool colour 8912
- Backing fabric
- Cushion pad

QUISQUALIS INDICA
FAMILY: COMBRETACEAE, QUISQUALIS PLANTS

Originally from Southeast Asia the Chinese honeysuckle grows so rapidly that it often has to be cut back to protect other plants in the garden. It is a very popular ornamental plant with flowers that grow on spikes that accumulate at the ends of the branches. The flowers have a long, very thin, stalk-like tube. Originally the flowers are white, then pink and finally crimson. Extracts of the leaves, roots and unripe fruits are thought to be an efficient treatment for eelworms.

INSTRUCTIONS

1 Follow the chart to work the design, starting from the middle. Use half cross stitch for the main part of the design.

2 Before starting the design for the border, first stitch a cross stitch around the central part of the design with the top part of the

cross going in the opposite direction to the half cross stitches. This will make the cross stitch stand out. Use two rows of canvas for the cross stitch.

3 Then stitch the border design using half cross stitch.

4 Finally, repeat the cross stitch around the edge of the design, again with the top of the cross facing in the opposite direction to the half cross stitches.

5 Press the embroidery on the back with a hot steam iron over a damp cloth and gently pull it back into shape. If it is still not straight dampen it again, pin it to a wooden board covered with a tea towel and leave to dry overnight.

6 With right sides together, sew the backing fabric to the embroidery on three sides.

7 Trim any excess canvas and fabric to within 13mm (½in). Also cut the corners diagonally.

8 Turn right sides out and insert the cushion pad.

9 Close the open seam with a slip stitch.

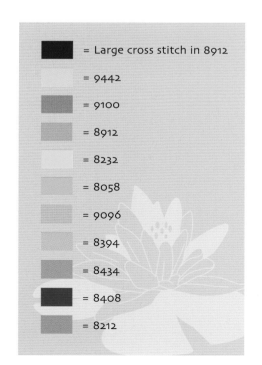

= Large cross stitch in 8912

= 9442

= 9100

= 8912

= 8232

= 8058

= 9096

= 8394

= 8434

= 8408

= 8212

A black and white version of this chart, which can be enlarged on a photocopier for easier working, can be found on p118

GOLDEN SHOWER CUSHION

MATERIALS

- 1 piece of 12 hole interlock canvas size 18 x 18in (46 x 46cm)
- 1 skein each of wool colours 9116, 9112, 8152, 9098, 8052, 8136, 8038, 8116, 9006, 9120
- 2 skeins of wool colour 8114
- 7 skeins of wool for background colour 9800
- Backing fabric
- Cushion pad

CASSIA FISTULA
FAMILY: CAESALPINIACEAE, CAROB PLANTS

The Golden Shower is a striking plant originally from India and Sri Lanka but now found in all tropical areas. The wonderful flowers usually grow to 30cm (12in) long but can be as long as 80cm (32in). They consist of different shades of yellow from very bright to pale. The plant has long leaves which tend to shed during the blooming period, although the tree is never entirely leafless. The sweet fleshy fruits of the Indian Golden Shower are sold as manna at the market and also act as a mild laxative. The fruits are long and thin, growing up to 24in (60cm). They are brown-black in colour with a roll of coin-like stacked seeds surrounded by a sticky brown pulp.

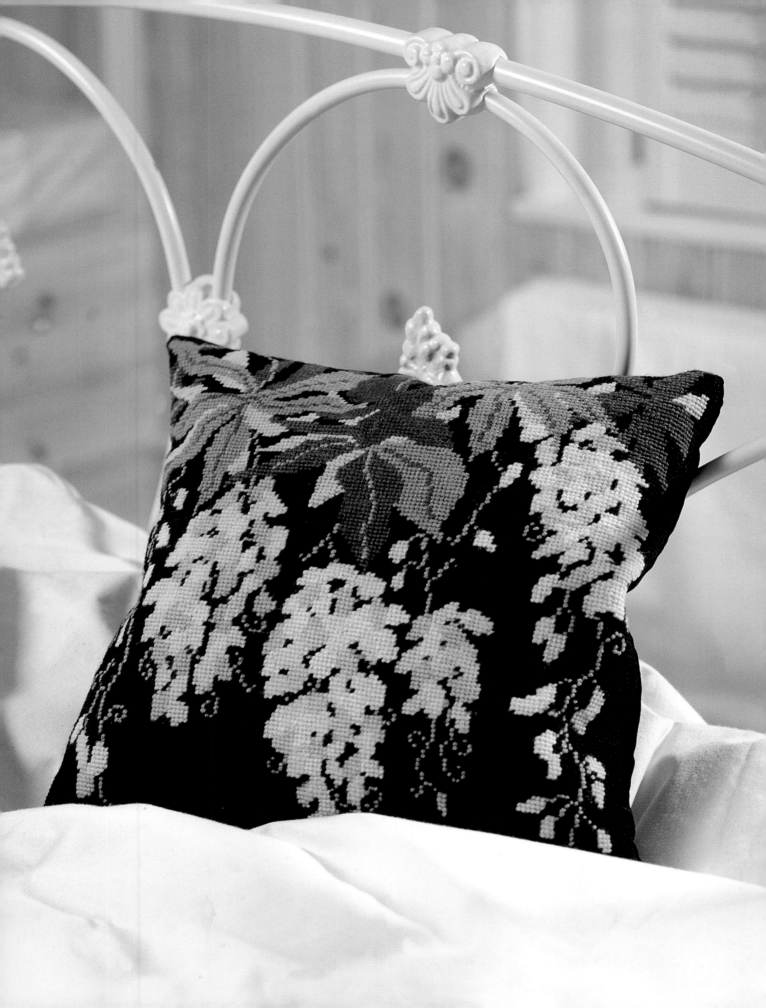

INSTRUCTIONS

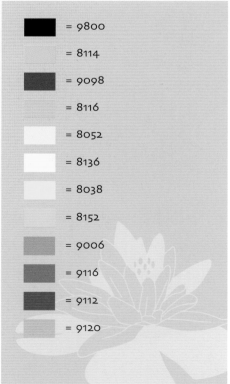

	= 9800
	= 8114
	= 9098
	= 8116
	= 8052
	= 8136
	= 8038
	= 8152
	= 9006
	= 9116
	= 9112
	= 9120

1 Follow the chart to work the design, starting from the middle. Use half cross stitch throughout.

2 Press the embroidery on the back with a hot steam iron over a damp cloth and gently pull it back into shape. If it is still not straight dampen it again, pin it to a wooden board covered with a tea towel and leave to dry overnight.

3 With right sides together, sew the backing fabric to the embroidery on three sides.

4 Trim any excess canvas and fabric to within 13mm (½in). Also cut the corners diagonally.

5 Turn right sides out and insert the cushion pad.

6 Close the open seam with a slip stitch.

A black and white version of this chart, which can be enlarged on a photocopier for easier working, can be found on p119

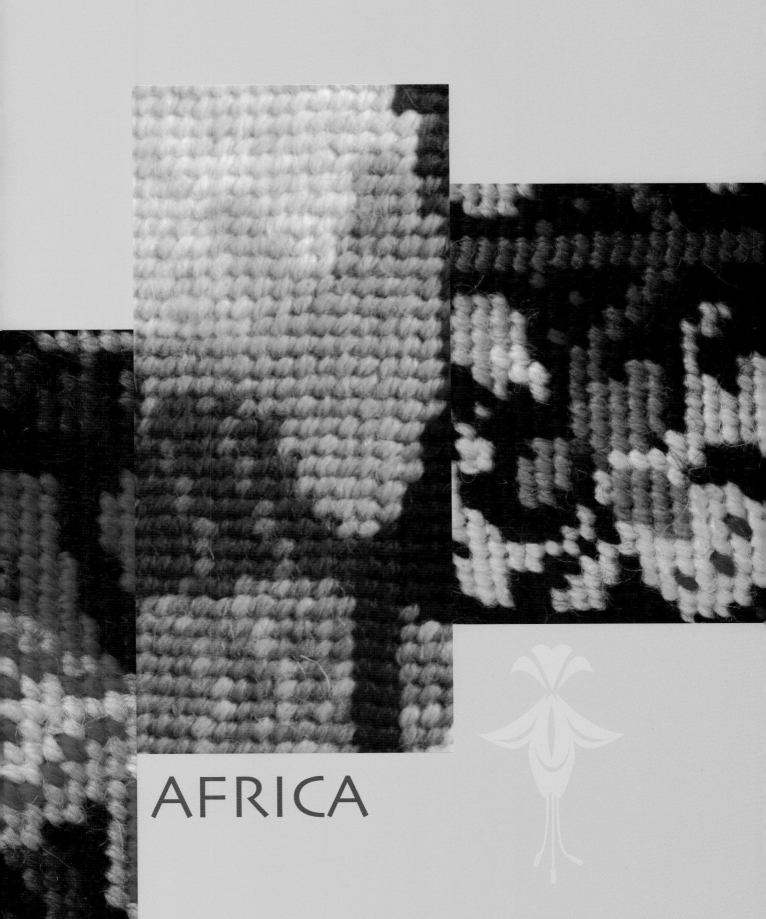

AFRICA

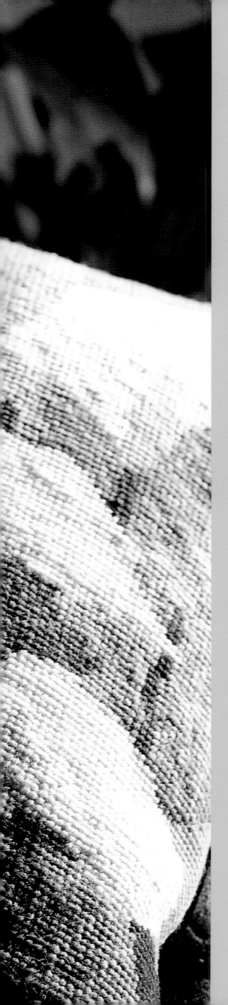

In Africa the tropical forests lie in pockets either side of the equator. In Central Africa it is predominantly in the Congo, in West Africa it is scattered along the Atlantic coast, and in East Africa there are small areas including the island of Madagascar. Again, massive deforestation is taking place with almost 90 per cent of Central and West Africa's rainforest already destroyed. These forests yield some of the world's most beautiful and valuable woods, such as teak, mahogany, rosewood, balsa and sandalwood; but it takes 60 years for a tropical rainforest tree to grow big enough to be used for timber. Madagascar is 2 per cent of Africa's land mass, but it has 10,000 species of plants with 80 per cent of them found nowhere else in the world. It is also the home to the world's lemurs, which are endangered.

One of the most remarkable features of tropical vegetation is the great number and variety of climbing plants. They can overgrow fences and bushes, wrap whole houses and tree trunks, hang in wide loops in forests or even grow erect in order to reach treetop level. Curtains of vines hiding everything behind them are typical in places where natural catastrophes have occurred or where man has cut strips into the forest. On the other hand, in undisturbed forests, vines usually grow in isolation. They use a wide variety of methods to reach the light, either using their supports to climb or winding their shoots around various supports. Vines usually start their growth in gaps and grow with the new forest up to the new height. In the treetops where branches intersect they can grow from tree to tree, and some vines have been measured at more than 1,970ft (600m) long. These have to have a very effective water system in their stems.

Because trees dominate the humid tropics, two very different biomes exist for bushes. One involves the shade of the forest, and the other involves deciduous growth. Usually, bushes that grow deep in the forest have either insignificant flowers, which rely completely on their fragrance to attract pollinators, or very bright, almost luminous flowers, which one can even see in the greenish twilight. In the case of deciduous growth, many different plants are competing for space, light and pollinators. Many have very remarkable flowers and are interesting as ornamental plants.

BLACK-EYED SUSAN PINCUSHION

MATERIALS
- 2 pieces of 12-hole interlock canvas size 8 x 8in (20 x 20cm)
- 1 skein each of wool colours 9800, 8114, 8116, 8168, 9098
- 2 skeins of wool colour 9120
- Padding

THUNBERGIA ALATA
FAMILY: ACANTHACEAE, ACANTHUS

The Black-eyed Susan is one of the few tropical plants that can be found in gardens in moderate climates, even if only as annual summer flowers. Originally from tropical Africa it is grown worldwide as an ornamental plant but will also grow wild as a weed. The plant loves sunny locations, needs a great deal of water and will tend to die off at the first frost. Besides the wild yellow specimen there are species with white and red flowers. Some of these do not have the typical dark centre. The Black-eyed Susan has herbaceous branches and can grow up to 13ft (4m) high.

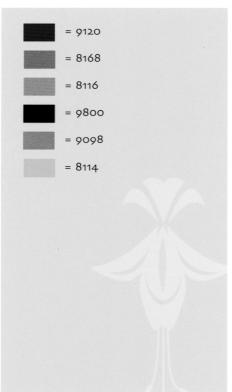

■	= 9120
■	= 8168
■	= 8116
■	= 9800
■	= 9098
■	= 8114

INSTRUCTIONS

1 Follow the chart to work the designs, starting from the middle. Use half cross stitch throughout.

2 Press the embroideries on the back with a hot steam iron over a damp cloth and gently pull them back into shape.

3 Trim any excess canvas to within 13mm (½in) and cut the corners diagonally.

4 Fold the unworked canvas to the wrong side all the way round.

5 With right sides facing out (wrong sides together), join the two pieces using a long-armed cross stitch starting just before one corner. Stitch almost all the way round leaving a gap of about 2in (5cm).

6 Stuff the pincushion and finally stitch the gap continuing the long-armed cross stitch.

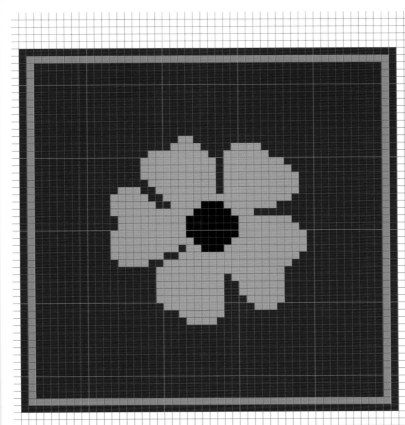

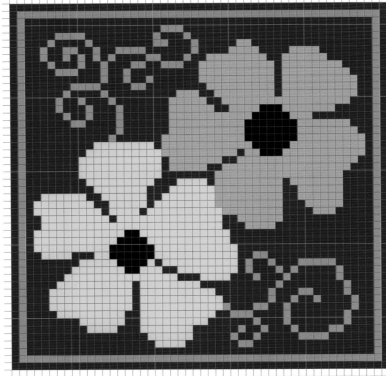

CARNIVAL BUSH
SPECTACLES CASE

MATERIALS

- 1 piece of 12-hole interlock canvas
  size 12 x 7in (30 x 18cm)
- 1 skein each of wool colours 8114,
  8016, 8152, 8490, 8204, 8198, 9018,
  9006, 9600, 9800
- Backing fabric
- Lining fabric

OCHNA SERRULATA
FAMILY: OCHNACEAE

This vibrant bush is frequently found in gardens but originated in the eastern part of South Africa. It is often cultivated for its bizarre fruits. Some people find the fruits reminiscent of Mickey Mouse with their spherical, black partial fruits, and one of the plant's other names is 'Mickey Mouse Tree'. Thee fruits are flower-shaped and backed by a bright red flower. The plant is richly branched and grows up to 10ft (3m) high, sometimes up to 20ft (6m). One particular variety of the carnival bush, the *Ochna arborea* grows even larger – up to 40ft (12m). Its heavy wood is used for tool handles and fence posts. A powder of its bark is inhaled for headaches, while the roots have also played a role in tribal medicines.

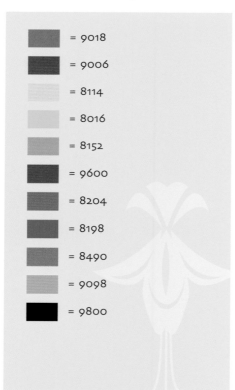

▇	= 9018
▇	= 9006
▇	= 8114
▇	= 8016
▇	= 8152
▇	= 9600
▇	= 8204
▇	= 8198
▇	= 8490
▇	= 9098
▇	= 9800

INSTRUCTIONS

1 Follow the chart to work the design, starting from the middle. Use half cross stitch throughout.

2 Press the embroidery on the back with a hot steam iron over a damp cloth and gently pull it back into shape.

3 Trim any excess canvas to within ½in (13mm). Also cut the corners diagonally.

4 With right sides together, sew the backing fabric to the embroidery leaving the top end open. Turn right sides out.

5 With right sides together, sew the lining fabric together leaving the top end open.

6 Put the lining inside the spectacles case and carefully sew around the open end, hiding any unworked canvas.

FLAMBOYANT SPECTACLES CASE

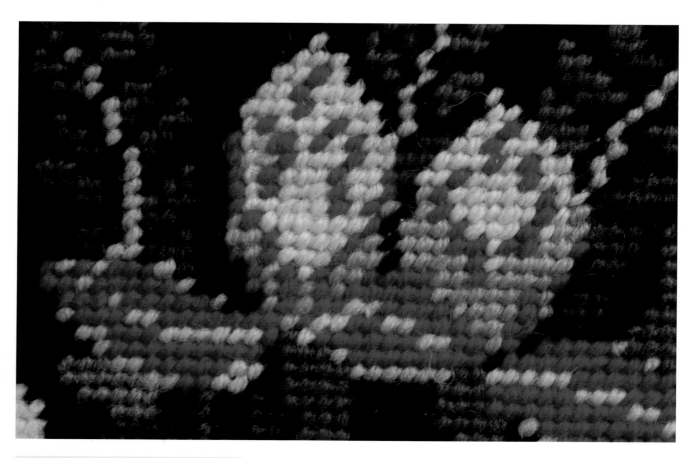

MATERIALS

- 1 piece 12-hole interlock canvas, size 12 x 8in (30 x 20cm)
- 1 skein each of wool colours 8006, 8392, 8434, 8216, 8114, 9006, 9014, 9018, 9022, 9800
- Backing fabric
- Lining fabric

DELONIX REGIA

FAMILY: CAESALPINIACEAE, CAROB PLANTS

The so-called flamboyant is one of the most striking tropical trees. Originally from Madagascar, it started to spread in the middle of the nineteenth century and now appears in many countries around the world. The flowers are orange to scarlet-red and 4–6in (10–15cm) long. Most appear at the end of the dry period together with new leaves. These trees may grow up to 50ft (15m) high but generally they are smaller than this. Day moths usually pollinate the flamboyant's flowers, but other insects and even birds also serve this purpose.

The American Cowslip.

INSTRUCTIONS

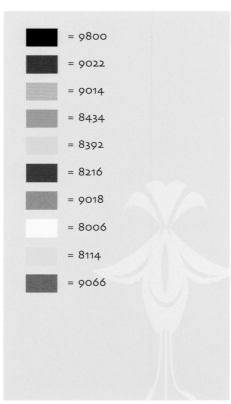

■	= 9800
■	= 9022
▨	= 9014
▨	= 8434
▨	= 8392
■	= 8216
▨	= 9018
□	= 8006
▨	= 8114
■	= 9066

1 Follow the chart to work the design, starting from the middle. Use half cross stitch throughout.

2 Press the embroidery on the back with a hot steam iron over a damp cloth and gently pull it back into shape.

3 Trim any excess canvas to within ½in (13mm). Also cut the corners diagonally.

4 With right sides together, sew the backing fabric to the embroidery leaving the top long end open. Turn right sides out.

5 With right sides together, sew the lining fabric together leaving the top long end open.

6 Put the lining inside the spectacles case and carefully sew around the open end, hiding any unworked canvas.

7 If desired this can be used as a purse by sewing poppers or a zip into the open sides.

CALLA LILY CUSHION

MATERIALS

- 1 piece 12-hole interlock canvas size 20 x 20in (50 x 50cm)
- 1 skein each of wool colours 8038, 9094, 9180, 9194, 9172, 8036, 8362, 9646, 9180
- 2 skeins each of wool colours 9006, 9100, 9016
- 3 skeins each of wool colour 8006, 8776
- Backing fabric
- Cushion pad

ZANTEDESCHIA AETHIOPICA
FAMILY: ARACEAE

The calla lily is an herbaceous plant with a firm rootstock. It grows 24–60in (60–150cm) high and was originally from South Africa although it is now cultivated in many tropical and subtropical areas. In addition, it can grow wild in marshy areas. Oddly enough, the calla lily is neither a 'calla', to which it is at best distantly related, nor a 'lily'. It thrives in any area where there is enough humidity and where there is not a frost that is strong enough to reach the rootstock hidden in the marsh. It is also a poisonous plant. As it tends to grow rapidly out of each fragment of its rootstock, in Australia and New Zealand it is considered a very undesirable weed.

	= 8776
	= 8036
	= 9094
	= 9016
	= 9194
	= 8038
	= 9172
	= 9100
	= 8362
	= 9194
	= 9006
	= 9180
	= 9646
	= 8006

INSTRUCTIONS

1 Follow the chart to work the design, starting from the middle. Use half cross stitch throughout.

2 Press the embroidery on the back with a hot steam iron over a damp cloth and gently pull it back into shape. If it is still not straight dampen it again, pin it to a wooden board covered with a tea towel and leave to dry overnight.

3 With right sides together, sew the backing fabric to the embroidery on three sides.

4 Trim any excess canvas and fabric to within ½in (13mm). Also cut the corners diagonally.

5 Turn right sides out and insert the cushion pad.

6 Close the open seam with a slip stitch.

A black and white version of this chart, which can be enlarged on a photocopier for easier working, can be found on p120

BLOODFLOWER PINCUSHION

MATERIALS

- 1 piece of 12-hole interlock canvas size 8in x 8in (20 x 20cm)
- 1 skein each of colour numbers 8132, 8392, 9100, 9006, 8114, 8216
- 2 skeins of colour number 9800
- Stuffing

ASCLEPIAS CURASSAVICA
FAMILY: ASCLEPIADACEAE, SILKWEED

The Bloodflower is widely spread as an ornamental plant and as a weed. It has large amounts of milky sap in all of its parts and it generally grows up to 4ft (1.2m). The hair of the seeds is too smooth and fragile to be useful. The plant is feared as a weed because it spreads very quickly. It is so poisonous that it is rarely eaten. Only the grubs of one insect (*Danaus chrysippus*) eat the leaves; they then become poisonous themselves. Butterflies often visit the flowers. In order to reach the nectar they stick their beaks into the coronas, get stuck, and transfer small packets of pollen.

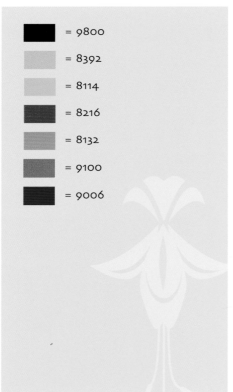

■	= 9800
	= 8392
	= 8114
	= 8216
	= 8132
	= 9100
	= 9006

INSTRUCTIONS

1 Follow the chart to work the designs, starting from the middle. Use half cross stitch throughout.

2 Press the embroideries on the back with a hot steam iron over a damp cloth and gently pull them back into shape.

3 Trim any excess canvas to within ½in (13mm) and cut the corners diagonally.

4 Fold the unworked canvas to the wrong side all the way round.

5 With right sides facing out (wrong sides together), join the two pieces using a long-armed cross stitch starting just before one corner. Stitch almost all the way round leaving a gap of about 2in (5cm).

6 Stuff the pincushion and finally stitch the gap continuing the long-armed cross stitch.

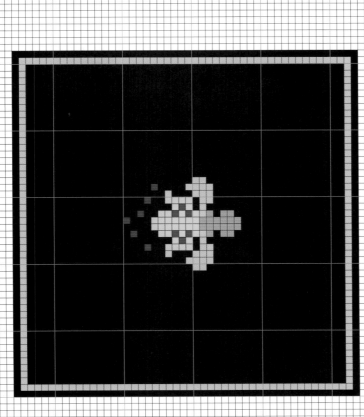

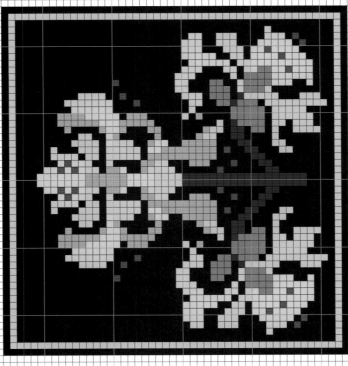

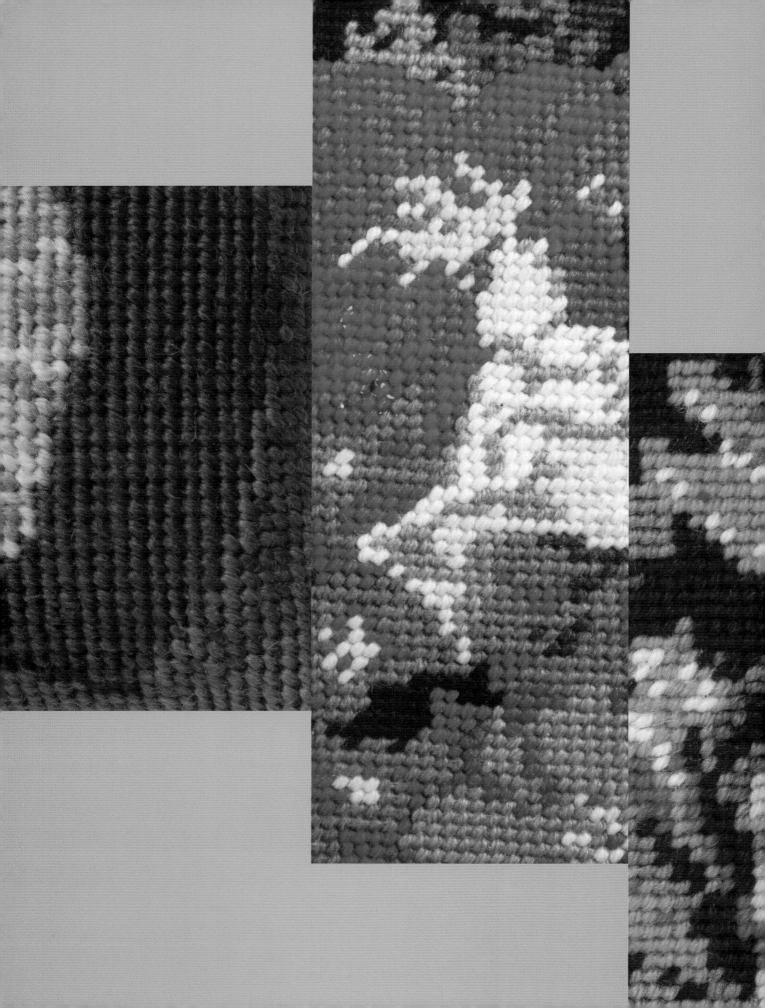

AMERICAS

The main rainforest areas of South America are to be found in the Amazonian region, extending northwards to the Caribbean, almost to the Tropic of Cancer and the Gulf of Mexico. Southwards the rainforest reaches the Tropic of Capricorn in Brazil, while to the west it climbs the foothills of the Andes and stretches beyond to the Pacific coasts of Colombia and Ecuador. South America is the home of the Amazon Basin and the Amazon river. This river is the world's largest and, its annual outflow accounting for one-fifth of all the fresh water that drains into the world's oceans. The water that doesn't make it to the river returns to the atmosphere through the process of transpiration. It has been found that half the rainfall in Amazonia returns to the atmosphere.

In the tropics the number of species is far higher than in moderate latitudes. An area of woodland containing ten species of trees in moderate latitudes would contain 180 species in a tropical forest. In addition, the variety of growth structures and the splendour of the many flowers are over-whelming. Tropical trees owe both facts to the lack of winter. This is the only reason that the blossoming time of a single species can continue throughout the year. The constant presence of nectar from their blossoms is a source of nutrients for larger animals such as birds and bats. Strong pollinators capable of long flights are advantageous because plants from any one species are often separated by long distances. Of course, bigger animals need larger blossoms with more nectar than do smaller insects. In addition, birds often have a poor sense of smell and, therefore, the blossoms must rely on the splendour of their colours to attract the necessary pollinators. One in five of all the birds on Earth live in Amazonia.

WILD AND CULTIVATED FLOWERS CUSHION

MATERIALS

- 1 piece of 12-hole interlock canvas
  size 20 x 16in (52 x 40cm)
- 1 skein each of wool colours 8006,
  8016, 8622, 8526, 8400, 8216,
  8644, 8690, 9526, 9172, 9006,
  9182, 9646, 9564, 9206
- 2 skeins each of wool colour 9800
- Backing fabric
- Cushion pad

This collection of wild and cultivated flowers includes the white-flowering *Portlandia grand flora*, the morning glory, orchids, the blue *Duranta erecta* and the *Hibiscus rosa-sinensis*. All making a colourful splash. Most tropical plants don't have English names – usually just the scientific name. Those that do have English names were developed from the English, German, French or Spanish names applied during the colonial period. Many of these folk names are not very specific. For example, if you wander across the country and asks for a 'buttercup orchid', you can be sure to be offered a dozen different species.

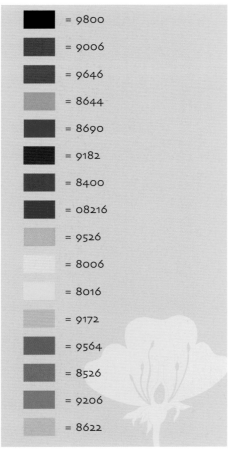

■	= 9800
■	= 9006
■	= 9646
■	= 8644
■	= 8690
■	= 9182
■	= 8400
■	= 08216
■	= 9526
■	= 8006
■	= 8016
■	= 9172
■	= 9564
■	= 8526
■	= 9206
■	= 8622

INSTRUCTIONS

1 Follow the chart to work the design, starting from the middle. Use half cross stitch throughout.

2 Press the embroidery on the back with a hot steam iron over a damp cloth and gently pull it back into shape. If it is still not straight dampen it again, pin it to a wooden board covered with a tea towel and leave to dry overnight.

3 With right sides together, sew the backing fabric to the embroidery on three sides.

4 Trim any excess canvas and fabric to within ½in (13mm). Also cut the corners diagonally.

5 Turn right sides out and insert the cushion pad.

6 Close the open seam with a slip stitch.

A black and white version of this chart, which can be enlarged on a photocopier for easier working, can be found on p121

SANTA CRUZ WATER LILY PINCUSHION

MATERIALS

- 2 pieces of 12 hole interlock canvas size 8 x 8in (20 x 20cm)
- 1 skein each of wool colours 8006, 8452, 8432, 9076, 9008, 9598, 9600, 9006
- 2 skeins of wool colour 8606
- Stuffing

VICTORIA CRUZIANA
FAMILY: NYMPHAEACEAE, WATER LILIES

The Santa Cruz water lily is not quite as famous as the Amazon water lily (*V. Amazonica*) but it is cultivated more frequently. It thrives in water temperatures that range from 20 to 25°C rather that the slightly higher temperatures of the Amazon water lily. The large floating leaves are one of the most important features of both lilies, ranging from 50 to 150cm (20–60in) wide. They are strong enough to support a small child. The flowers grow individually on the surface of the water. They are 25–35cm (10–14in) wide and have many petals and stamens which blend into one another. The flowers are white at first then change to dark pink. The Santa Cruz water lily is widely cultivated in bodies of standing water. It is native to Paraguay, the southern part of Brazil and the northern part of Argentina.

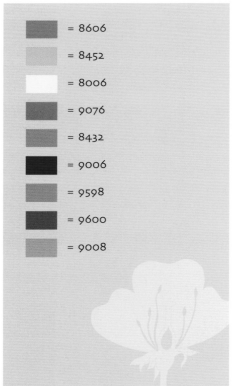

▨	= 8606
▨	= 8452
▨	= 8006
▨	= 9076
▨	= 8432
▨	= 9006
▨	= 9598
▨	= 9600
▨	= 9008

INSTRUCTIONS

1 Follow the chart to work the designs, starting from the middle. Use half cross stitch throughout.

2 Press the embroideries on the back with a hot steam iron over a damp cloth and gently pull them back into shape.

3 Trim any excess canvas to within 13mm (½in) and cut the corners diagonally.

4 Fold the unworked canvas to the wrong side all the way round.

5 With right sides facing out (wrong sides together), join the two pieces using a long-armed cross stitch starting just before one corner. Stitch almost all the way round leaving a gap that is about 2in (5cm).

6 Stuff the pincushion and finally stitch the gap continuing the long-armed cross stitch.

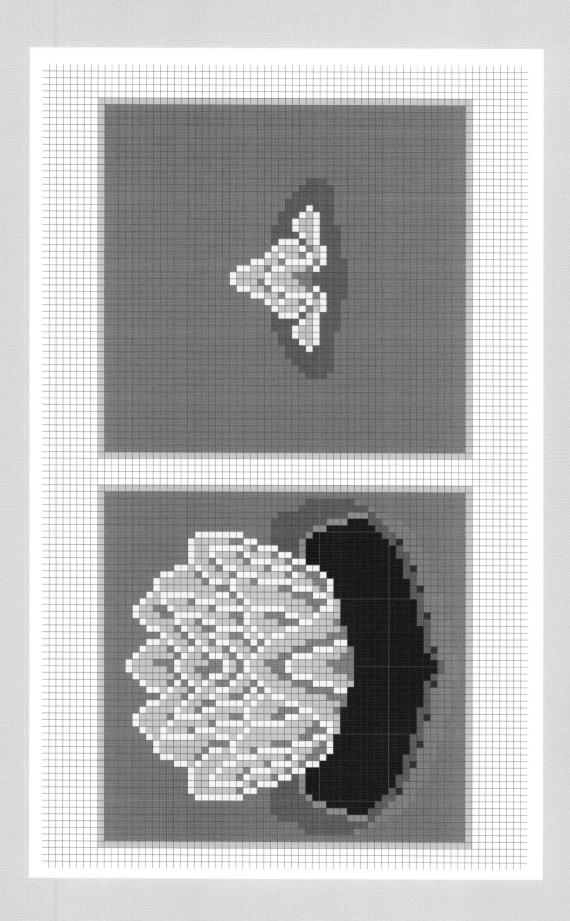

BRAZILIAN WILDFLOWER PICTURE

DELONIX REGIA
FAMILY: CAESALPINIACEAE, CAROB PLANTS

MATERIALS

- 1 piece of 10 hole double thread canvas size 20 x18in (50 x 45cm)
- 1 skein each of 8006, 8218, 8228, 9640, 8016, 9534, 8162, 9018, 9100, 9020, 9182
- 2 skeins of 8644
- 3 skeins of 9646
- Picture frame if desired or a piece of thick cardboard

These wild flowers are indigenous to the highlands of Brazil. They include *Bignonia venusta* and *Quamoclit nationis* climbing over a forest tree. Plants that grow on other plants are called 'epiphytes'. These differ from parasites in that they do not penetrate into their host in order to withdraw water and nutrients. Instead they use them only as a surface. If they damage their hosts at all, it is because both plants are competing for space and light. Epiphytes are able to reach the light using only a small amount of nutrients and energy. However, they are exposed to the weather and have to withstand strong winds, hefty rain showers, cold night-time temperatures and the burning heat of the sun.

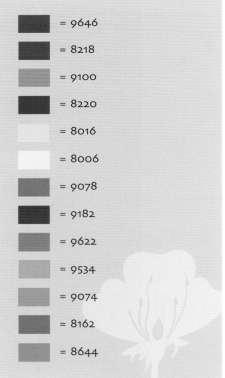

■	= 9646
■	= 8218
■	= 9100
■	= 8220
■	= 8016
■	= 8006
■	= 9078
■	= 9182
■	= 9622
■	= 9534
■	= 9074
■	= 8162
■	= 8644

INSTRUCTIONS

1 Follow the chart to work the design, starting from the middle. Use half cross stitch throughout.

2 Press the embroidery on the back with a hot steam iron over a damp cloth and gently pull it back into shape. If it is still not straight dampen it again, pin it to a wooden board covered with a tea towel and leave to dry overnight.

3 Position the embroidery over a thick piece of card cut slightly smaller than the finished needlepoint.

4 Carefully lace the excess canvas together, firstly side to side and then top to bottom.

5 If desired, the picture can now be framed.

A black and white version of this chart, which can be enlarged on a photocopier for easier working, can be found on p122

MORNING GLORY BELL PULL

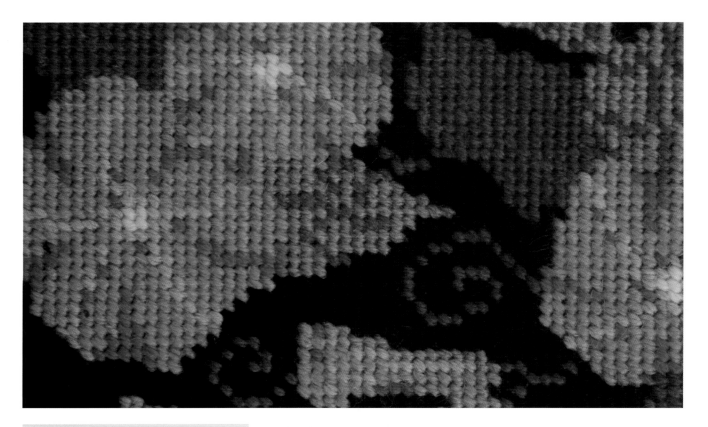

MATERIALS
- 1 piece of 10 hole double thread canvas size 49 x 9in (123 x 23cm)
- 1 skein each of wool colours 8690, 8114, 8490, 9218
- 2 skeins each of wool colours 9018, 9006, 8990
- 3 skeins each of wool colour 8486
- 4 skeins each of wool colour 8644
- 10 skeins each of wool colour 9800
- Backing fabric
- Bell-pull fixings
- Tassel

IPOMOEA PURPUREA
FAMILY: CONVOLVULACEAE, BINDWEED

This plant, otherwise known as morning glory, grows with herbaceous shoots up to 16ft (5m) high. It winds up trees and can grow so rapidly that it often turns into a problem. There are approximately 650 species of morning glory, most of which have simple heart-shaped leaves. This one, the *Ipomoea purpurea*, is a wild specimen with blue-violet flowers and a light to white tube. It has reddish stripes in the middle of the corolla lobes. The flowers tend to grow individually or in small groups. Generally one can find the morning glory everywhere in the tropics, including along roadsides and on fallow land. Its origin is uncertain.

INSTRUCTIONS

1 Follow the chart to work the design. Instead of starting in the middle, it may be easier to start at the top left-hand corner of the design and work down. Use half cross stitch throughout.

2 Stitch the design as shown on the chart, then work two full repeats. Work a third repeat leaving out the curved vine next to the blue flower at the bottom of the design.

3 Press the embroidery on the back with a hot steam iron over a damp cloth and gently pull back into shape.

4 With right sides facing and stitching as close to the stitches as possible, sew the lining to the embroidery down the two long sides only.

5 Trim back any excess canvas and fabric along those edges, ensuring that you leave 13mm (½in) allowances, and turn the work right side out.

6 Sew the bell-pull fixings to the top and bottom of the bell pull.

7 Trim back any further excess canvas and lining. Turn in the edges and finish sewing across the two shorter edges of the bell pull.

8 Stitch a tassel to the bottom bell-pull fixing.

= 9800
= 8644
= 8690
= 8486
= 8114
= 8490
= 9018
= 9218
= 8990
= 9006

PASSION FRUIT PINCUSHION

MATERIALS

- 2 pieces of 12-hole interlock canvas size 8 x 8in (20 x 20cm)
- 1 skein each of wool colours 8006, 8014, 8052, 9172, 8296, 9096, 8198, 9598, 8168, 8166, 8434
- Stuffing

PASSIFLORA CAERULEA
FAMILY: PASSIFLORACEAE, PASSIONFLOWER

Originally from South America, the passion flower can be found throughout the world. It climbs with tendrils and can reach up to 50ft (15m). The plant is woody at ground level and the flowers are very individual, having five calyxes and five corollas, and look wonderfully exotic. They are about 4in (10cm) in diameter and the ten white petals and sepals are surmounted by a mass of radiating filaments that are purple toward the centre of the flower, becoming white and finally lavender-purple at the tips. The fruits are spherical to ovate with a tough peel that is dark purple or yellow. The juice pressed from the coat of the seeds of the passion fruit can be drunk. Many of the approximately 430 passion flower species are cultivated but all need full sun and plenty of water when in growth during the summer months.

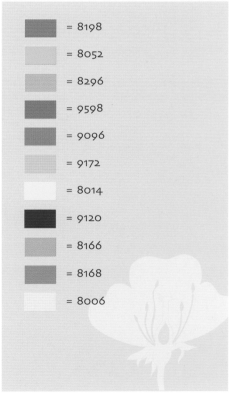

■	= 8198
■	= 8052
■	= 8296
■	= 9598
■	= 9096
▤	= 9172
□	= 8014
■	= 9120
■	= 8166
■	= 8168
▤	= 8006

INSTRUCTIONS

1 Follow the chart to work the designs, starting from the middle. Use half cross stitch throughout.

2 Press the embroideries on the back with a hot steam iron over a damp cloth and gently pull them back into shape.

3 Trim any excess canvas to within ½in (13mm) and cut the corners diagonally.

4 Fold the unworked canvas to the wrong side all the way round.

5 With right sides facing out (wrong sides together), join the two pieces using a long-armed cross stitch starting just before one corner. Use wool number 8434 as an exciting contrast. Stitch almost all the way round leaving a gap about 2in (5cm).

6 Stuff the pincushion and finally stitch the gap continuing the long-armed cross stitch.

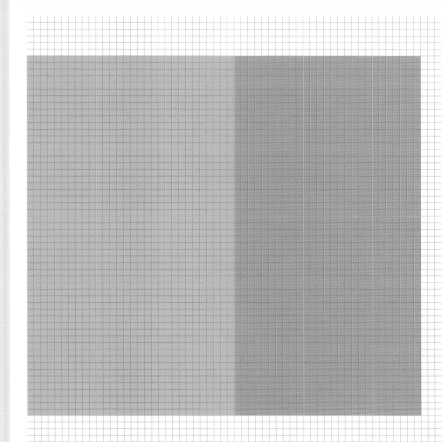

CULTIVATED CROPS

In the tropics agriculture occupies large areas. For example, the oil-palm plantations in Malaysia or the rice fields in Thailand stretch over many hundreds of square kilometres. The immense variety of flora in the tropics is reflected in agriculture, where the number of species grown is well over a thousand. Under natural conditions these plants are easily pushed aside into deep shadow, and some, like the ginger and banana plants, can sometimes reach treelike dimensions. They are usually grown in free fields or in light forest.

In the closed forest, leafy plants often have strikingly coloured or sculpted leaves. As much as this may look like a game of nature, it is important for the survival of the plants. The red colourings in the leaves help plants to use the energy-rich blue light which is able to reach the ground. Plants need this blue light because the chlorophyll in the tallest trees has already absorbed the red light, which normally starts the process of photosynthesis. Strongly sculpted leaves improve the rate of evaporation, helping to carry nutrients through the plants, though this is difficult in the humid air on the ground in the forest.

Rainforests are home to more species of plants than the rest of the world put together. An astounding number of fruits (bananas, citrus), vegetables (peppers, okra), nuts (cashews, peanuts), drinks (coffee, tea, cola), oils (palm, coconut), flavourings (cocoa, vanilla, sugar, spices), and other foods (beans, grains, fish) come from rainforests. Tropical forest oils, gums and resins are found in insecticides, rubber products, fuel, paint, varnish and wood-finishing products, cosmetics, soaps, shampoos, perfumes, disinfectants and detergents. Over 2000 rainforest plants have been shown to have anti-cancer properties.

Although the rate of deforestation is incredible, with at least 42 million acres of tropical forest lost each year (which equates to approximately 100 acres a minute), there have been a couple of successful projects. In 1990 Brazil's President Jose Sarney signed laws allowing more than five million acres of forest to be managed by rubber tappers, nut gatherers and others whose livelihood depends on the rainforest harvest. And in Papua New Guinea, butterfly farms are a successful operation that provides income and supports forest preservation.

COFFEE PLANT SPECTACLES CASE

MATERIALS

- 1 piece of 12-hole interlock canvas size 7 x 10in (18 x 26cm)
- 1 skein each of wool colours 8006, 8296, 8216, 8218, 8220, 9602, 9016, 9006, 8992, 8688
- Backing fabric
- Lining fabric

COFFEA ARABICA
FAMILY: RUBIACEAE

Coffee is one of the most important cultural plants. Approximately 25 million people earn their living from coffee and about one-third of people on earth drink it. The coffee beans are the seeds of the coffee berry. The fruity flesh is removed right after the harvest but the beans are not roasted until they reach the consumer country. Besides Arabian coffee, which provides almost three-quarters of worldwide production, two other species are cultivated: Robusta coffee and Liberian coffee. Robusta coffee accounts for most of the remaining production and comes from a species that grows at lower altitudes. Liberian coffee only represents about one per cent of the worldwide market. Arabian coffee is a small tree that grows up to 20ft (6m) high with horizontal branches. When cultivated it is often kept as a bush. It has wonderfully aromatic flowers, with five to eight growing together in a bunch. Originally from the Ethiopian highlands, this tree is grown in many tropical countries, often under shade trees at altitudes ranging from 2000–4000ft (600–1200m).

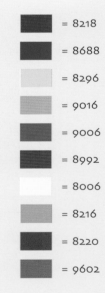

■	= 8218
■	= 8688
■	= 8296
■	= 9016
■	= 9006
■	= 8992
□	= 8006
■	= 8216
■	= 8220
■	= 9602

INSTRUCTIONS

1 Follow the chart to work the design, starting from the middle. Use half cross stitch throughout.

2 Press the embroidery on the back with a hot steam iron over a damp cloth and gently pull it back into shape.

3 Trim any excess canvas to within 13mm (½in). Also cut the corners diagonally.

4 With right sides together, sew the backing fabric to the embroidery leaving the top end open. Turn right sides out.

5 With right sides together, sew the lining fabric together leaving the top end open.

6 Put the lining inside the spectacles case and carefully sew around the open end, hiding any unworked canvas.

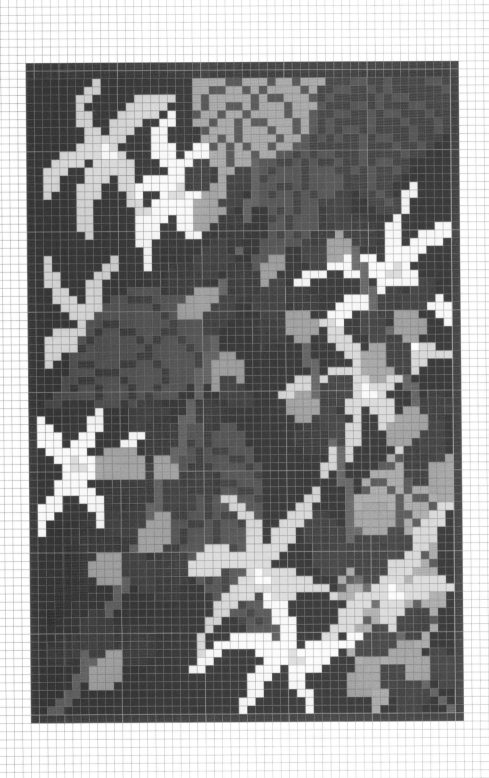

CAYENNE PEPPERS CUSHION

MATERIALS

- 1 piece of 12 hole interlock canvas size
- 1 skein each of wool colours 8006, 8114, 8392, 8644, 9646, 9076, 9100, 9006, 9096, 9104
- 3 skeins each of wool colour 8216
- 5 skeins each of wool colour 8740
- Backing fabric
- Cushion pad

CAPSICUM ANNUUM
FAMILY: SOLANACEAE, SOLANUM

The cultivated specimens of *Capsicum annuum* provide such a variety of fruits that one has a hard time recognizing them as the offspring of one single species. They range from small and very spicy, such as the chilli specimens, to the oblong cayenne pepper, up to the large, spherical, mild bell pepper. These plants are cultivated almost all over the world as annuals, but they play a special role in the tropics because their spiciness stimulates the appetite, even in great heat. The cayenne pepper plant is short and broad. It is richly branched, often having two or three lateral branches next to each flower with small leaves in the axils of the larger ones. The flowers are greenish-white to pale violet, and the fruits are hollow with curved seeds. This plant is cultivated worldwide. Originally it was from the Western hemisphere.

■	= 8216
■	= 8740
■	= 9104
■	= 8644
▦	= 9096
▦	= 8114
■	= 9100
■	= 9600
□	= 8006
■	= 9646
▦	= 8392
■	= 9076

INSTRUCTIONS

1 Follow the chart to work the design, starting from the middle. Use half cross stitch throughout.

2 Press the embroidery on the back with a hot steam iron over a damp cloth and gently pull it back into shape. If it is still not straight dampen it again, pin it to a wooden board covered with a tea towel and leave to dry overnight.

3 With right sides together, sew the backing fabric to the embroidery on three sides.

4 Trim any excess canvas and fabric to within ½in (13mm). Also cut the corners diagonally.

5 Turn right sides out and insert the cushion pad.

6 Close the open seam with a slip stitch.

A black and white version of this chart, which can be enlarged on a photocopier for easier working, can be found on p123

CASHEW NUT CUSHION

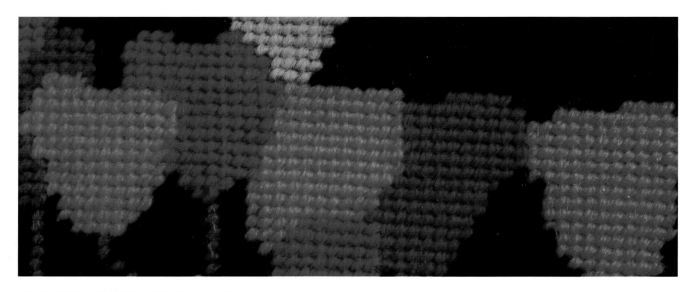

MATERIALS

- 1 piece 12-hole interlock canvas size 16 x 16in (40 x 40cm).
- 1 skein each of colour number 8442, 8214, 8202, 9100, 9600
- 2 skeins each of colour number 9156, 9006, 9196
- 4 skeins of 9800
- Backing fabric
- Cushion pad

ANACARDIUM OCCIDENTALE

FAMILY: ANACARDIACEAE, SUMACH PLANTS

The cashew nut tree has a variety of uses. In earlier times people ate the fleshy fruit stalk. The nut was more or less ignored because its shell contains a poisonous oil that irritates the skin. However, this was used in folk medicine. Today the oil is used to produce paints, varnish and brake and clutch linings. After roasting, the nut becomes deliciously edible, containing 45 per cent fat and 20 per cent protein. Cashew nut trees grow in all tropical areas. They originated in Central America, the Caribbean and the northern part of South America. The tree itself is usually small, seldom growing higher than 50ft (15m). Often it is cultivated as a bush. The flowers grow at the ends of the numerous branches. They have five petals that change colour in the flowering season from greenish-white to pink. The fruits are divided into two parts and hang down. One part is up to 4in (10cm) long and is fleshy and shaped somewhere between an apple and a pear. The other, much smaller part is only about 1in (2.5cm) long and is kidney-shaped. It is brown with a hard peel that covers the seeds.

INSTRUCTIONS

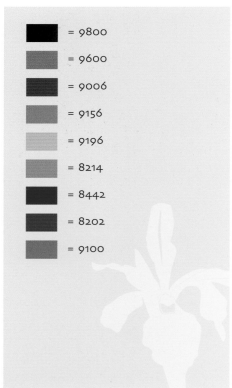

	= 9800
	= 9600
	= 9006
	= 9156
	= 9196
	= 8214
	= 8442
	= 8202
	= 9100

1 Follow the chart to work the design, starting from the middle. Use half cross stitch throughout.

2 Press the embroidery on the back with a hot steam iron over a damp cloth and gently pull it back into shape. If it is still not straight dampen it again, pin it to a wooden board covered with a tea towel and leave to dry overnight.

3 With right sides together, sew the backing fabric to the embroidery on three sides.

4 Trim any excess canvas and fabric to within ½in (13mm). Also cut the corners diagonally.

5 Turn right sides out and insert the cushion pad.

6 Close the open seam with a slip stitch.

A black and white version of this chart, which can be enlarged on a photocopier for easier working, can be found on p124

COCONUT PALM BOOKMARK

MATERIALS

- 1 piece 12-hole interlock canvas size 10 x 6in (25 x 15cm)
- 1 skein each of wool colours 9600, 9646, 8688, 8690, 8164
- 1 skein each of stranded cotton colour 246
- 1 piece of card cut slightly smaller than the embroidery
- Small tassel
- Lining fabric

COCOS NUCIFERA
FAMILY: ARECACEAE PALMS

The coconut palm is an extremely important plant because of its usefulness – no part remains unused. The trunk provides wood, the leaves become materials for roofing and weaving, the flowers or inflorescences give a sweet juice for many things including sugar and palm wine itself and finally the fruit has many uses. These coconuts have a thick fibrous cover with a leathery exterior shell. This gives the fruit its buoyancy; fruits have been found after drifting for 4500km (2800 miles) in the ocean over a four-month period. Inside the coconut the nut contains a firm white sugary edible fibre which can be turned into dried coconut and coconut oil. In addition, the younger nuts contain a clear, refreshing fluid called coconut milk. The latter is not actually in the nut, it develops when ground-up edible fibre is filled with hot water and the water is pressed out.

LITTLE BIRD RED.

Here is a treat for every one;
Now eat away till all are done.
I stay with you, whilst mother
    dear
Can fly amid the thicket near;
She'll like, I know, to flit about,
And find the fresh wild straw-
    berries out.

LITTLE BIRD BLUE.

Farewell! I'll bring you home
    the best,
And soon be back, to go to rest.

SECOND SCENE.

SWALLOW.

O GRIEF! what have I lived to
    see?

ROBIN.

Speak out—what has befallen
    thee?

SWALLOW.

Some cruel boy a snare has laid,
Little Bird Blue is prisoner made.

27

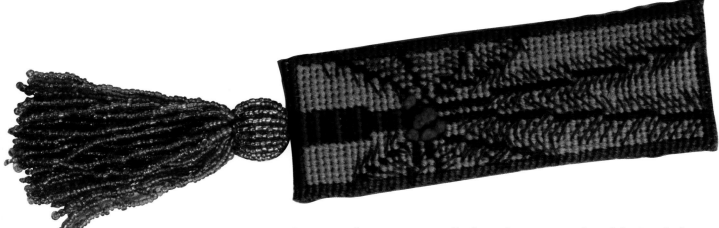

Coconut palms were originally from the western edge of the Pacific but now can be found naturally along coasts across the globe and are often planted inland. They can grow up to 100ft (30m) high with the trunk usually in the shape of an arch – seldom straight unless cultivated. The fruits are greenish to orange-yellow and up to 12in (30cm) long.

INSTRUCTIONS

1 Follow the chart to stitch the design starting in the middle.

2 Make large French Knots for the coconuts in colour 8164.

3 Press the embroidery on the back with a hot steam iron.

4 With two strands of thread in the needle in stranded cotton colour 246, overstitch the wool to make the leaves. It doesn't need to be too exact.

5 Place the finished embroidery over the card and fold the excess canvas behind the card. Lace the excess pieces together with some spare wool.

6 Add a tassel if required.

7 Carefully slip-stitch the lining to the back of the embroidery.

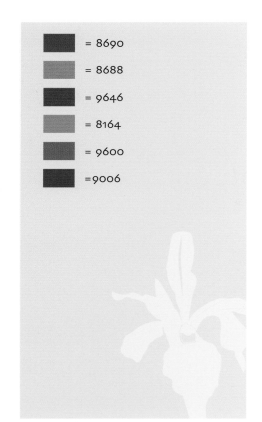

= 8690
= 8688
= 9646
= 8164
= 9600
=9006

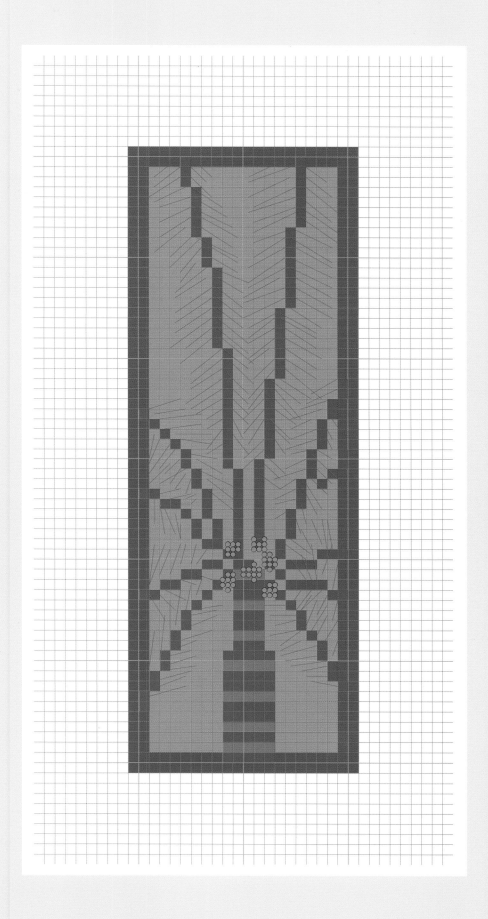

GLOBE ARTICHOKE CUSHION

MATERIALS

- 1 piece 12-hole interlock canvas size 16 x 16in (42 x 42cm)
- 1 skein each of wool colours 8252, 9372, 9638, 9308, 8052, 8488, 9006, 9016
- 6 skeins each of wool colour 9800
- Backing fabric
- Cushion pad

CYNARA SCOLYMUS
FAMILY: ASTERACEAE

The globe artichoke is from the family of large thistles originally from the Mediterranean, which are now grown as a vegetable and found throughout the world. The plant is less silvery than its relations but the leaves can reach 24–28in (60–70cm) in length. In summer, tall branched woolly stems support large $3\frac{1}{2}$in (8cm) wide purple flowers at a height of up to 5ft (1.5m) or more. The leaf-stalks on the head are eaten after being blanched, but if left the thistle-like flowers are magnificent to see.

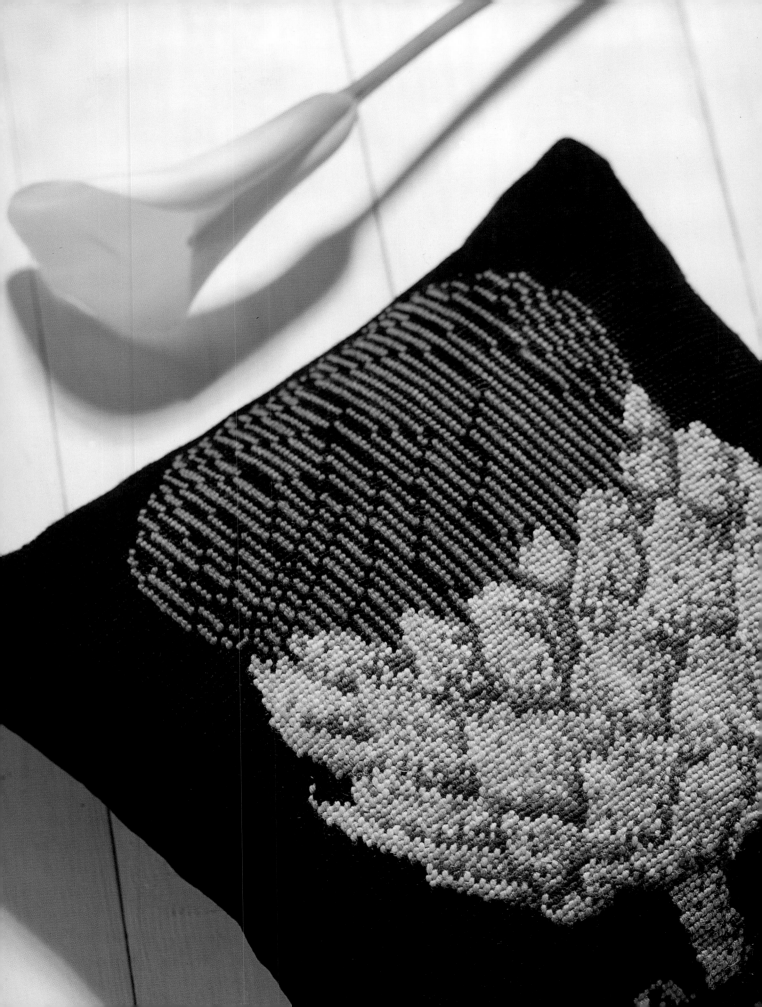

INSTRUCTIONS

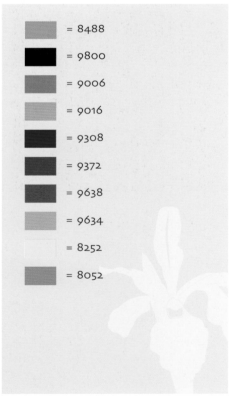

▇	= 8488
▇	= 9800
▇	= 9006
▇	= 9016
▇	= 9308
▇	= 9372
▇	= 9638
▇	= 9634
▇	= 8252
▇	= 8052

1 Follow the chart to work the design, starting from the middle. Use half cross stitch throughout.

2 Press the embroidery on the back with a hot steam iron over a damp cloth and gently pull it back into shape. If it is still not straight dampen it again, pin it to a wooden board covered with a tea towel and leave to dry overnight.

3 With right sides together, sew the backing fabric to the embroidery on three sides.

4 Trim any excess canvas and fabric to within 13mm (½in). Also cut the corners diagonally.

5 Turn right sides out and insert the cushion pad.

6 Close the open seam with a slip stitch.

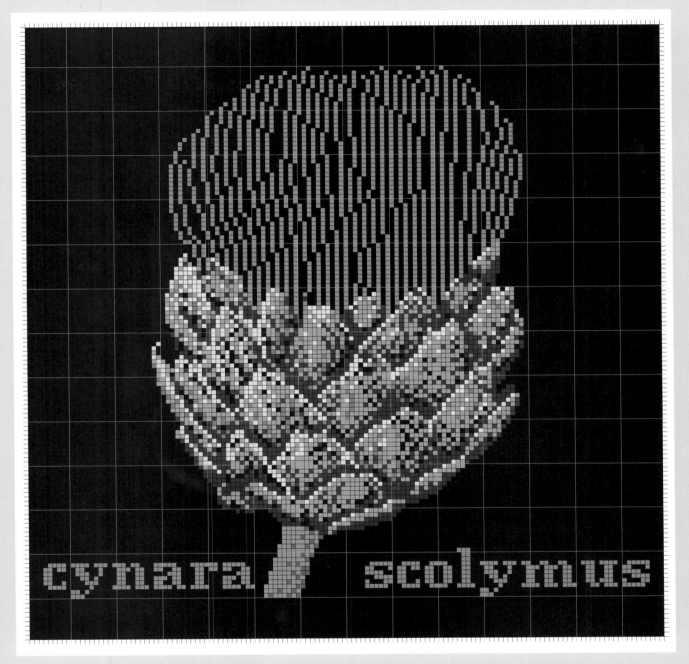

A black and white version of this chart, which can be enlarged on a photocopier for easier working, can be found on p125

PINK AND BLUE TROPICAL FLOWERS CUSHION, P27

MALAYSIAN ORCHID TREE CUSHION, P31

CHINESE HONEYSUCKLE CUSHION, P39

GOLDEN SHOWER CUSHION, P43

CALLA LILY CUSHION, P63

WILD AND CULTIVATED FLOWERS CUSHION, P75

BRAZILIAN WILDFLOWER PICTURE, P83

CAYENNE PEPPERS CUSHION, 103

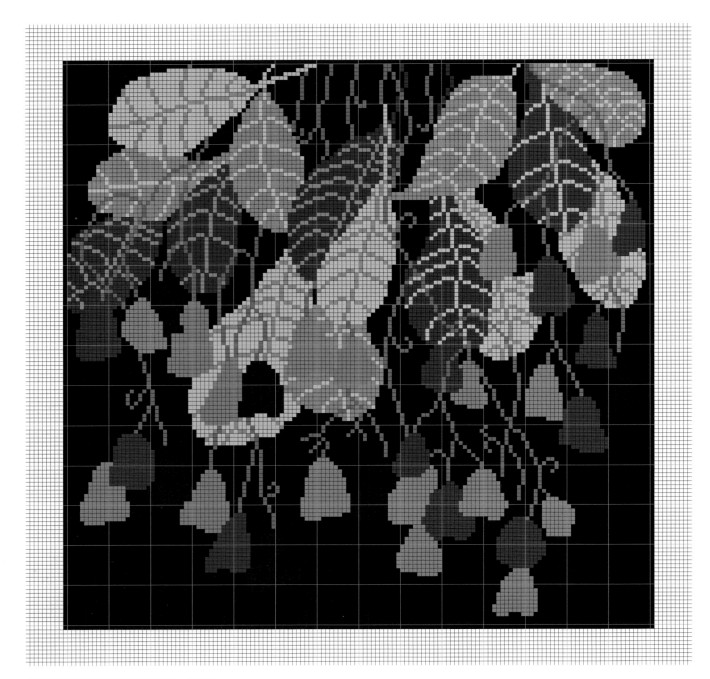

CASHEW NUT CUSHION, P107

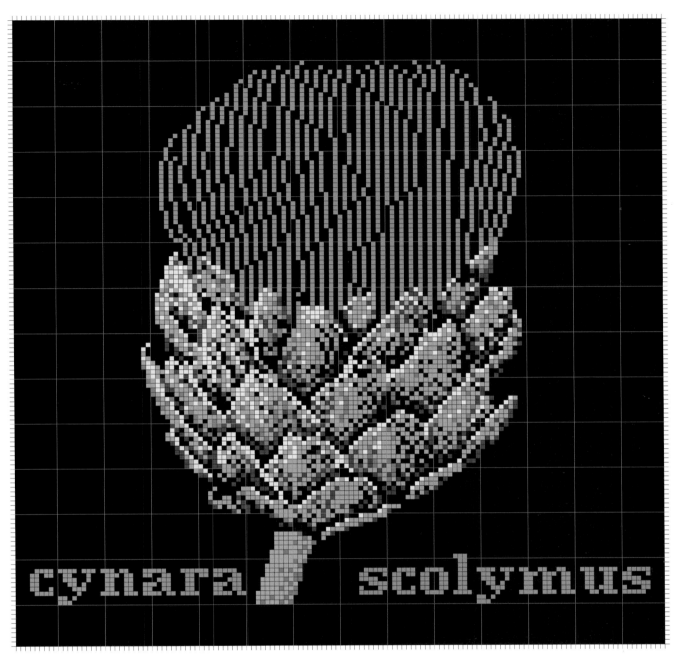

GLOBE ARTICHOKE CUSHION, P114

THREAD CONVERSION CHART

This conversion chart is for guidance only, as exact comparisons are not always possible.

Anchor	DMC	Madeira	Anchor	DMC	Madeira	Anchor	DMC	Madeira	Anchor	DMC	Madeira
1	blanc	2401	162	825	1107	330	947	205			
6	353	2605	164	824	2505	332	946	207	894	3326	813
8	3824	304	185	964	1112	333	608	206	895	223	812
10	351	406	186	959	1113	334	606	209	896	315	810
13	347	211	188	943	2706	335	606	209	897	221	2606
19	817	407	189	991	2705	337	922	403	899	3022	1906
20	3777	2502	205	912	1213	341	355	314	903	3032	2002
22	815	2501	206	564	1210	343	932	1710	905	3021	1904
35	3705	411	214	368	2604	349	301	2306	968	778	808
38	3731	611	215	320	1310	351	400	2304	969	816	809
45	814	2606	216	367	1310	352	300	2304	970	3726	2609
46	6566	210	217	319	1312	357	975	2602	1012	948	305
47	304	510	227	701	1305	358	801	2008	1014	355	2502
49	3689	607	236	3799	1713	359	898	2007	1021	963	404
50	605	613	241	703	1307	360	938	2005	1023	760	405
52	957	2707	245	701	1305	368	436	2011	1024	3328	406
54	956	611	246	986	1404	369	435	2010	1025	347	407
68	3687	604	253	772	1604	371	433	2602	1027	223	812
69	3685	2609	254	3348	1409	372	738	2013	1036	336	1712
70	*	2608	255	907	1410	376	842	1910	1037	3756	2504
74	3354	606	256	906	1411	378	841	2601	1042	369	1701
75	3733	505	264	3348	1409	379	840	2601	1070	993	
76	961	505	265	471	1308	380	838	2005	1072	993	
78	600	2609	266	470	1502	382	3371	2004	1074	3814	
85	3609	710	267	469	1503	386	746	2512	1089	996	
94	917	706	268	937	1504	390	822	1908	1090	996	
97	554	711	269	895	1507	397	3204	1901	5975	356	401
99	552	2714	276	3770	2314	398	415	1802	1335		
101	550	713	278	472	1414	400	317	1714	1345		
102	*	2709	279	734	1610	403	310	2400			
108	210	2711	280	581	1611	683	890	1705			
109	209	2711	289	307	103	781					
112	*	2710	292	3078	102	842	3013	1605			
117	341	901	293	727	110	843	3012	1606			
118	340	902	295	726	109	846	936	1507			
122	3807	2702	297	973	105	847	928	1805			
127	823	1008	298	972	107	850	926	1707			
137	798	911	300	677	111	856	370	1509			
139	797	912	303	742	114	858	524	1512			
140	3755	910	305	743	109	871	3041	806			
145	799	910	306	725	2514	876	503	1703			
146	798	911	307	783	2514	877	502	1205			
147	797	912	309	781	2213	878	501	1205			
149	336	1006	311	977	2301	879	500	1204			
150	823	1007	314	741	203	885	739	2014			
152	939	1009	316	740	202	887	3046	2206			
160	813	1105	323	722	307	888	3045	2112			
161	826	1012	326	720	309	889	610	2105			

INDEX